GREEN GOLD ANIMATION PVT. LTD.

PRESENTS

CHHOTA BHEEM™

VOL . 56

in

MAGIC PUPPETS

Created By: Rajiv Chilaka

Story: Nidhi Anand

AF663682

A puppeteer comes to Dholakpur and manages to impress the people of the village with his show. He is very generous with the kids and gives away free puppets.

Soon, the village is being robbed of its gold. Where is all the gold going?

Is the puppeteer involved in this? Will Bheem solve this mystery? Enjoy this fun filled magical adventure!

www.greengold.tv

www.chhotabheem.com

Hi! I am **Bheem.** I am a brave, strong, intelligent and fun loving nine year old and I love laddoos. They give me super human strength. I also love helping the poor and needy.

Hello everybody!! I am **Chutki,** a seven-year-old girl. I am generous, sweet, graceful, intelligent and happy natured and I love to accompany Bheem in helping people. My mother owns the laddoo shop from which Bheem gets his favourite laddoos.

Hey guys! I am **Raju.** I am a very cute, brave and tough four year old and Bheem is my hero. My father is a soldier in the king's army and I love to play war games with Bheem.

Hello! I am Bheem's friend and the talking monkey. People call me **Jaggu.** I am clever and funny and I love to accompany Bheem everywhere. I love to play tricks on Dholu-Bholu and Kalia and all the kids love me because I entertain them.

Hi everybody! We are **Dholu-Bholu,** the identical twins who fear and follow Kalia. We are dumb and we keep getting ourselves into trouble. We get bribed by laddoos easily and become disloyal to Kalia occasionally.

Hey all! I am the hefty, strong and arrogant ten-year-old boy, **Kalia.** I am jealous of Bheem and always try to put him down. I love to bully kids younger and weaker than me. I have two silly followers who are Dholu and Bholu.

ONE FINE MORNING, A "PUPPET SHOW" WAS ORGANIZED FOR THE PEOPLE OF DHOLAKPUR
PUPPET SHOW
EVERYONE FROM ELDERS TO CHILDREN, GATHER TO SEE THE SHOW WITH GREAT EXCITEMENT
PUPPET SHOW
HURRY! THE SHOW IS GOING TO START
EVERYONE IS EAGERLY WAITING FOR THE PUPPET SHOW TO BEGIN
THANK GOD! WE ARE ON TIME
HEY! THE WHOLE VILLAGE SEEMS TO BE HERE
YES CHUTKI! YOU ARE RIGHT

THE PUPPETEER APPEARS IN FRONT OF THE AUDIENCE TO PERFORM
LADIES AND GENTLEMEN, WELCOME TO THE GREAT "PUPPET SHOW"
WHY IS HE TAKING SO LONG TO START?
HERE YOU GO MY PUPPETS!
PULL
RIPP
THE CURTAIN IS RAISED...
SRUPP
SRUPP
...AND THE PUPPET APPEARS IN FRONT OF THE CROWD
PULL
SILENCE PLEASE!
PULL
RIPP
RIPP
THE SHOW IS GOING TO BEGIN
PULL
RIPP
WE WERE JUST GETTING READY
PULL
RIPP

THE PROBLEM IS THAT MY WIFE TAKES A LONG TIME TO GET READY
DO NOT WORRY. SHE WILL BE HERE SOON
HA HA HA!
HA HA HA!
HO! HO! HO!
WHAT DID YOU SAY? YOU ARE COMPLAINING TO THE KIDS ABOUT ME?
UH! WHO'S VOICE WAS THAT?
IT WAS THE PUPPET'S WIFE WHO WAS RUNNING BEHIND HIM
OH NO! SHE HAS HEARD IT ALL. I AM DONE FOR!
OH NO! SHE IS NOT GOING TO SPARE ME
PULL
RIPP
HEY YOU! STOP THERE
AAAH!
RIPP
PULL
RIPP
WAIT! WHERE ARE YOU GOING?
PULL
RIPP
PULL

IT WAS A FUN SHOW WITH THE WIFE GOING BEHIND HER HUSBAND!
SWOOM
EXCUSE ME! I WILL BE RIGHT BACK
COME BACK
AHH!!!
ZOOM
HEY STOP!
ZOOP
THE CURTAINS ROLL DOWN
IT IS TIME FOR A SMALL BREAK
PULL
RIPP
GOOD SHOW!
CLAP CLAP
CLAP CLAP
WHAT A WONDERFUL SHOW!
WE WANT MORE
THANK YOU, THANK YOU! SO MUCH

HERE THEY GO AGAIN!
THE CURTAINS PART ONCE AGAIN...
SRUPP
SRUPP
...AND ALL THE PUPPETS COME DOWN DANCING
THEY ARE BACK AGAIN!
HA, HA! THEY LOVE MY SHOW!
RIPP
PULL
WOW! AMAZING
GREAT
OUR LITTLE RAJU WAS A BIT CONFUSED
CHUTKI, HOW ARE THESE PUPPETS WALKING AND TALKING?

DO THEY HAVE SOME MAGICAL POWERS IN THEM?
NO NO RAJU! THERE IS NO MAGIC, LOOK CAREFULLY...
...THE PUPPETS ARE TIED TO STRINGS. WHEN THE PUPPETEER PULLS THEM...
RIPP
PULL
RIPP
PULL
PULL
PULL
RIPP
...IT LOOKS AS THOUGH...
...THE PUPPETS ARE...
...MOVING AND DANCING
TAP!
TAP!
TAP!
FINALLY...
...THE SHOW COMES TO AN END AND THE CROWD CLAPS AND WHISTLES
CLAP
CLAP
OKAY KIDS! THAT IS ALL FOR TODAY!
RIPP
PULL

I HOPE YOU ALL ENJOYED THE SHOW. BYE BYE!
THE CURTAINS CLOSE AND...
...THE THRILLED CROWD COMES OUT AMIDST MUCH EXCITEMENT
I ENJOYED A LOT DAD!
WOW! WHAT AN IMPRESSIVE SHOW IT WAS
GREAT SHOW!
THE PEOPLE OF DHOLAKPUR COULD JUST NOT STOP TALKING ABOUT THE WHOLE EVENT
WOW!
AH!
A LITTLE BOY STARTS TO PESTER HIS FATHER
I WANT A PUPPET!
NO DEAR, DO NOT BE STUBBORN
UNLESS YOU GIVE ME A PUPPET...
AAAH!!!
...I WILL NOT GO HOME
THE PUPPETEER WAS WATCHING THE BOY SOB
!?
DO NOT BE STUBBORN
BOO! HOO! HOO!
BOO! HOO! HOO!

DO NOT CRY MY CHILD
YOU CAN TAKE THIS
AH!
B... BUT?
THIS PUPPET IS ALL YOURS
TAKE IT MY BOY
THE LITTLE BOY HAPPILY TAKES AWAY THE PUPPET WITH HIM
YEAH YEAH!
KEEP IT. IT IS A GIFT FROM ME
THANK YOU! SO MUCH
HERE IS YOUR MONEY...
NO, NO I CANNOT TAKE IT

LOOK HOW HAPPY HE IS
THERE IS NO PRICE FOR A CHILD'S HAPPINESS
THAT IS REALLY VERY KIND OF YOU THANK YOU!
JUST THEN
EVEN I WANT A PUPPET
OH! NO NO NO
BOO HOO HOO!
COME ON, DO NOT CRY
THE PUPPETEER GENEROUSLY GIVES AWAY HIS PUPPET TO THE LITTLE GIRL
HERE TAKE IT
A PUPPET FOR YOU TOO!
AAAH!
HA HA HA!
HEY! YIPEE!
I GOT IT I GOT IT
HA HA HA!
HA HA HA!

DHOLAKPUR LOOKED BEAUTIFUL UNDER THE STARLIT SKY
THE LITTLE GIRL WAS VERY EXCITED
LET US PLAY
HMM... WHAT DO I CALL YOU?
UH!? COME ON DEAR
IT IS QUITE LATE
PUT THAT PUPPET IN THE BOX NOW AND GO TO SLEEP
OK MOTHER, BUT I WILL KEEP IT ALONG WITH ME
OKAY!
GOOD NIGHT DEAR!
AND SOON THE LITTLE GIRL ALONG WITH HER PUPPET WAS FAST ASLEEP
PHOO
PHOO

NEXT MORNING...
COCK-OO-DOODLE-DOO
...AT THE LITTLE GIRL'S HOUSE
BAAAW!
IT IS MORNING ALREADY...
HUH, WHAT IS THIS?
OH! NO MY CHAIN
THE LITTLE GIRL'S MOTHER IS IN SHOCK AND...
...RUSHES OUT TO MEET TUNTUN AUNTY
HEY! LISTEN
WHAT HAPPENED?
LAST NIGHT WHEN I WENT TO SLEEP...

...THE GOLD CHAIN WAS AROUND MY NECK. BUT WHEN I WOKE UP TODAY, IT WAS GONE
OH!?
I HAVE SEARCHED THE WHOLE HOUSE THRICE BUT HAVE NOT FOUND IT
OH REALLY! SOMETHING SIMILAR HAPPENED WITH MY NEIGHBOUR TOO
SHE TOO COULD NOT FIND HER EAR RINGS
!?
!?
EH! EVEN MY WIFE'S BRACELET...
...GOT LOST LAST NIGHT
THE VILLAGERS WERE PUZZLED AND DECIDED TO MEET THE KING
O' KING! SOMETHING STRANGE IS HAPPENING IN OUR VILLAGE
GOLD ORNAMENTS HAVE BEEN MISSING FROM OUR HOUSES...
...AND NONE OF US HAS EVEN SEEN A THIEF...

...OR ANY TRACES OF THE THEFT BEING DONE
HMMMM... THIS IS INDEED VERY STRANGE
YES, MY LORD I CANNOT REALLY UNDERSTAND...
...THERE HAS NOT BEEN A SINGLE BROKEN DOOR OR WINDOW...
...IT IS HARD TO EXPLAIN WHICH WAY THE THIEF IS USING TO GET IN AND OUT OF HOUSES
IF THIS IS THE CASE...
...THEN I SHALL APPOINT MY SOLDIERS IN EVERY CORNER OF DHOLAKPUR, TONIGHT...
...WHOEVER THE THIEF MAYBE HE WILL SURELY BE CAUGHT
BHEEM, I WOULD LIKE YOU TO STAY ALERT WITH THE SOLDIERS TONIGHT, AND HELP THEM TO NAB THE THIEF
DO NOT WORRY MY MAJESTY, I WILL DO MY BEST

IT WAS A DARK NIGHT FULL OF GLITTERING AND SPARKLING STARS
LET ME SEE IF I CAN FIND SOME CLUE
HMMM...
ZZZZZZZZ
ZZZZZZZZ
ZZZZZZZZ
DO YOU THINK THE THIEF WILL COME?
AH!
HEY, LOOK THERE BHEEM!
DOINK
JAGGU SEES SOMEBODY RUNNING ON THE ROOF OF THE HOUSES
LISTEN TO ME CAREFULLY. YOU GUYS GO FROM FRONT...
...AND WE WILL KEEP A WATCH FROM BEHIND, IN CASE HE TRIES TO ESCAPE FROM THE BACK
NOW QUICK TAKE YOUR POSITIONS
SHHH... KEEP YOUR VOICE DOWN
AHA!!!
CAUGHT YOU, WHERE WILL YOU ESCAPE NOW?

IT IS YOU!
BUT TO BHEEM'S SURPRISE, IT WAS KALIA
KALIA YOU?
EH! YOU?
HUH! IT WAS YOU, I THOUGHT...
...I CAUGHT THE THIEF
WHAT WERE YOU DOING ON TOP OF THE ROOF?
I THOUGHT IF THE THIEF DOES NOT BREAK DOORS AND WINDOWS...
...THEN HE MUST BE USING THE ROOF. BUT I FOUND NO ONE THERE TOO
OH NOO!!!
HHMMPP!!! BHEEM WHAT DO WE DO NOW?

THE SUN WAS SHINING BRIGHTLY THE NEXT MORNING IN THE BEAUTIFUL SKY
AAW!!! IT IS MORNING ALREADY
JUST THEN A WOMAN COMES OUT OF HER HOUSE IN A HURRY
OH NO!
MY EAR RINGS ARE MISSING
AAH!!!
I AM NOT FINDING MY GOLD BANGLES TOO!
MEANWHILE BHEEM ALONG WITH KALIA AND JAGGU REACHES THERE
TELL ME EXACTLY WHAT HAPPENED?
OUR BANGLES AND EAR RINGS ARE MISSING
BUT HOW CAN THIS BE POSSIBLE?
NO ONE ENTERED ANY HOUSE, NEITHER DID ANYONE COME OUT...
...SO HOW IS THE GOLD VANISHING?

EH!?
OH!?
JUST THEN
THE PUPPETEER COMES THERE
COME KIDS, COME HERE
HEY LOOK, WHAT I HAVE GOT FOR YOU
ALL THE KIDS WERE VERY EXCITED TO SEE THE PUPPETEER
AHA!
WOW!
AHA!
I HAVE GOT THESE PRETTY CLOTHES...
...FOR YOUR PUPPETS
THEY WILL LOOK BRIGHT AND BEAUTIFUL ON THEM
GIVE IT TO ME
THE PUPPETEER QUICKLY TAKES THE PUPPET...
...AND TURNS AROUND TO CHANGE THE PUPPET'S DRESS
HERE I GO
TAKE MY PUPPET TOO

NOW, THEY LOOK WONDERFUL IS NOT IT?
WOW AMAZING!!!
SOON ALL THE PUPPETS HAVE NEW DRESSES
COME KIDS, TAKE YOUR PUPPETS
THANK YOU!
YIPPEE! NEW CLOTHES FOR MY PUPPET
LOOK AT THE DIFFERENCE
THERE THAT THIEF IS ROBBING US...
...AND HERE IT IS YOU WHO IS BUSY DISTRIBUTING THE PUPPETS FREE OF COST
!?
PLEASE TAKE SOME MONEY FOR THESE PUPPETS
NO NO, MONEY DOES NOT MATTER...

...I AM SO THRILLED TO SEE THESE KIDS HAPPY
HA HA HA HA!
BHEEM IS SUSPICIOUS OVER THE PUPPETEER'S BEHAVIOUR
THIS IS VERY STRANGE
THIS PUPPETEER NOT ONLY GIFTS HIS PUPPETS TO THE KIDS...
...BUT ALSO KEEPS MAKING FREE THINGS FOR THEIR PUPPETS
BHEEM, THE THEFTS HAVE ALSO BEGUN SINCE...
...THIS PUPPETEER CAME HERE
WHY DO NOT WE FOLLOW HIM AND FIND OUT WHAT THE MATTER IS?

LATER THAT NIGHT BHEEM AND HIS FRIENDS MADE THEIR WAY TO THE PUPPETEER'S TENT
SHHH...
PUPPET SHOW
THEY SLOWLY PEEP INSIDE THE TENT
THERE IS NO-ONE HERE
SHH... LET US GO AND SEE BEHIND THE CURTAIN
ALL OF THEM WERE SHOCKED TO SEE...
OH NOO... WHAT IS HE UPTO?
AAH!
AAH!
...THAT THE PUPPETEER WAS PERFORMING SOME KIND OF MAGIC ON ALL THE PUPPETS!
WAKE UP, WAKE UP...
...WAKE UP MY PUPPETS...
...WAKE UP, WAKE UP
IT IS NIGHT NOW

TIME TO WAKE UP
THE MAGIC SPELL WORKS ON THE PUPPETS...
...AND THEY ALL START TO RISE
OH! SO THIS IS THE MATTER!
BHEEM SLOWLY SNEAKS OUT OF THE CURTAIN
COME ON LET US GO
BUT WHERE?
TONIGHT, WE DON'T HAVE TO GUARD THE HOUSES FROM OUTSIDE...
...INSTEAD WE WILL HAVE TO PEEP INSIDE
HURRY! LET'S NOT WASTE TIME

BHEEM PEEPS THROUGH THE WINDOW OF A HOUSE
CREEK
CREEK
EVERYBODY IN THE HOUSE WAS FAST ASLEEP
ZZZZZ...
ZZZZZ...
ZZZZZ...
SUDDENLY THE MAGIC PUPPET GETS UP...
...AND WALKS STRAIGHT TOWARDS THE WOMAN
ZZZZZ...
ZZZZZ...
THE PUPPET PULLS AWAY THE CHAIN FROM HER NECK...
PULL
OH! LOOK AT THAT
...AND GOES BACK TO SLEEP
I FINISHED MY WORK
THIS MEANS, WHEN THE PUPPETEER COMES EVERYDAY WITH NEW CLOTHES...
...HE CHANGES THEM AND QUIETLY TAKES OUT THE GOLD

COME, LET US GO AND TEACH HIM A LESSON
NO, WAIT RAJU. THE VILLAGERS THINK HE IS VERY GENEROUS
SO, HE SHOULD BE EXPOSED IN FRONT OF EVERYONE
NEXT DAY
COME KIDS, COME HERE
HEY! IT IS OUR FAVORITE UNCLE AGAIN!
LET US GO!
LOOK I HAVE BROUGHT ALL THESE NEW CLOTHES
WOW! THEY ARE SO COLOURFUL
WAIT UNTIL I RUIN ALL YOUR PLANS, YOU CHEAT!
HE IS HERE AGAIN!
OH NO!
UNAWARE OF THE PUPPETEER'S EVIL INTENTIONS, EVERYONE GATHERS AROUND HIM
COME ONE, COME ALL

HEY, THIS IS FOR YOUR PUPPET
SEE, HOW WELL HE ACTS
GIVE IT TO ME
THE PUPPETEER TURNS AROUND TO CHANGE THE PUPPET'S OLD DRESS INTO A NEW ONE
HUH! THEY WILL NEVER KNOW
HE SOON TAKES AWAY THE GOLD HIDDEN IN THE CLOTHES OF THE PUPPET
ALL THIS IS MINE!
JUST A MINUTE...
AND THEN
...HERE YOU GO
EVERYBODY KEENLY LOOKS AT THE PUPPETEER'S ACT
HUH! WHAT AN ACTOR!

BHEEM WAS WAITING FOR THE RIGHT TIME TO EXPOSE THE TRUE CHARACTER OF THE PUPPETEER
THANK YOU! THANK YOU! IT LOOKS SO PRETTY
HUH?
GIVE ME YOUR PUPPET
HERE YOU GO
IT WAS FINALLY TIME FOR EVERYONE TO KNOW THE TRUTH ABOUT THE PUPPETEER
JAGGU, IT IS YOUR TURN TO ACT
JAGGU SLOWLY SNEAKS BEHIND THE PUPPETEER WHILE...
...A FEW KIDS NOTICE IT
AAH!?
HEY!
IT IS TIME FOR SOME FUN!
HE SLOWLY SLIPS A MOUSE...
...IN THE PUPPETEER'S DRESS
HERE YOU GO!

KIDS, JUST A MINUTE, IT IS ALMOST DONE
HOW DID YOU LIKE IT?
HE HE HE!
HA! HA! HA!
AND THEN SUDDENLY
UMPHHH!
!?
OH NO! WHAT IS WRONG WITH THIS PUPPETEER
UH!?
EEKS!
WHAT IS HAPPENING?
HA! HA! HA!
IT IS NOT OVER YET
SERVES HIM RIGHT
HA! HA! HA!
THE PUPPETEER WAS STILL NOT AWARE THAT...
AAH!

...A MOUSE WAS IN HIS DRESS
SCRATCH! SCRATCH!
SCRATCH! SCRATCH!
OH NO!
SCRATCH! SCRATCH!
SCRATCH! SCRATCH!
JUST THEN
THWAPP
CLINK! CLINK!
CLING! CLING!
CLING! CLING!
EVERYONE IS SURPRISED TO SEE THE GOLD JEWELS FALL FROM THE PUPPETEER'S CLOTHES
WHAT IS ALL THIS?
EIKKSSS!
EVERYONE WAS VERY ANGRY
GRRR!
GRRR!
GRRR!
GRRR!
EEYOW!
AAAH!
AAAH!
EEEKS!
SCRATCH!
SCRATCH!
FINALLY THE MOUSE COMES OUT...
...AND HE TAKES A SIGH OF RELIEF
BOING!
AH! NOW I FEEL BETTER

HE QUICKLY GETS UP AND TRIES TO...
GRINNN!
...ESCAPE
WHOOPS!
WHOOSH!
EH! I BETTER RUN FAST
ZOOM
AHA! NOT SO FAST
AAGHH!
TAKE THIS
KAPOW!
OWW... OWWW... OUCH!!! WHERE AM I?
DOINK
DOINK
THANK YOU SO MUCH BHEEM!
PANT... PUFF...
ONCE AGAIN OUR MIGHTY HERO CHHOTA BHEEM ALONG WITH HIS FRIENDS WISELY SOLVED THE PROBLEM OF THE VILLAGERS
HA! HA! HA! HA! HA!
WELL DONE BHEEM
HURRAY! HURRAY!
THE END

CHHOTA TAB, BADA MAZZA!
India's first Android Tablet just for kids.
CHHOTA BHEEM tab
EARLY LEARNING FOR KIDS
Chhota Bheem tab brings you entertainment, fun and learning - all in one! With premium preloaded nursery rhymes, storybooks, learning apps, videos and games as well as access to plenty of exciting downloads. Grab your tab and let the fun begin!
Award-winning Design
7" Screen
Parental Controls
Expandable Storage
Kids-Safe App Store
Tough, Durable Design
www.chhotabheemtab.com | toll free: 1800 200 2334
MOSTI

CHHOTA BHEEM COMIC BOOKS

Vol 01.WHERE IS BHEEM
Vol 02.BABBAN SHER
Vol 03.THE SEA PRINCESS
Vol 04.THE WOOD CUTTER
Vol 05.CROCODILE KRAZZY
Vol 06.CIRCUS IN DHOLAKPUR
Vol 07.SAMURAI SAM
Vol 08.TALKING PARROT
Vol 09.GOLD
Vol 10.THE GIANT
Vol 11.THE LOST ALIEN
Vol 12.HYPNOTIST HARRY
Vol 13.EINSTEIN BHEEM
Vol 14.FLYING CARPET
Vol 15.ROCKY THE RHINO
Vol 16.THE INVISIBLE MAN
Vol 17.TRIBE
Vol 18.COWBOY BHEEM
Vol 19.BULL RACE
Vol 20.THE MUMMY
Vol 21.20-20 CRICKET
Vol 22.SHIVANI KA DHABA
Vol 23.THE SWORD
Vol 24.DHOLAKPUR ATHLETICS CHAMPIONSHIP
Vol 25.USO AT DHOLAKPUR
Vol 26.EVIL MINISTRATIONS
Vol 27.DIWALI DHAMAKA
Vol 28.THE GENIE'S OUT OF THE BOTTLE
Vol 29.GIRLS VS GIRLS
Vol 30.CHOCOLATE WORLD
Vol 31.INDUMATI'S BIRTHDAY
Vol 32.CHHOTA BHEEM & GANESH
Vol 33.KING FOR A DAY
Vol 34.QUEEN CHUTKI
Vol 35.THIS IS NOT THE RIGHT SIZE
Vol 36.SUPER HERO
Vol 37.THE DOLPHINS
Vol 38.TREE HOUSE
Vol 39.REVENGE OF THE ANTS
Vol 40.THE GIRAFFE
Vol 41.KALIA'S PET
Vol 42.LADDOO NO. 1
Vol 43.THE GLADIATOR
Vol 44.THE KARATE TWINS
Vol 45.BOARD GAME
Vol 46.HOLI HAI
Vol 47.THE FRANKENSTEIN
Vol 48.BOOK OF WORLD RECORDS
Vol 49.JUNIOR BOXING CHAMPIONSHIP
Vol 50.THE KINGFISHER
Vol 51.CAMPING HOLIDAY
Vol 52.EVIL DRUMMER
Vol 53.BLAST FROM THE PAST
Vol 54.JUNGLE PARTY
Vol 55.JUNGLE BOY
Vol 56.MAGIC PUPPETS
Vol 57.TOUCH OF STONE
Vol 58.THE MAGIC CHALK
Vol 59.TALKING TEDDY
Vol 60.SEA WORLD
Vol 61.HIDING GAME
Vol 62.JAGGU DAGGU BHAI BHAI
Vol 63.CRUISE TO ICELAND
Vol 64.HAPPY NEW YEAR
Vol 65.DHOLU BHOLU
Vol 66.ALIBABA'S CAVE
Vol 67.KALIA'S MASTER PLAN
Vol 68.COME BACK
Vol 69.DAAKU KA CHACHU
Vol 70.TREASURE HUNT - II
Vol 71.THE TALISMAN
Vol 72.KHUSTI KA MUQABLA
Vol 73.THE CONFUSED CAMEL
Vol 74.THE GOOD WITCHE'S LAND
Vol 75.FUN SCHOOL
Vol 76.MISSING: HAVE YOU SEEN THESE KIDS?
Vol 77.DUMDAAR DADAJI
Vol 78.SABSAY FILMY
Vol 79.INDUMATI AND THE FROG PRINCE
Vol 80.BHEEM AND THE CHIPMUNKS
Vol 81.PUPPY LOVE
Vol 82.BUBBLE TRAP
Vol 83.WATER TO GOLD
Vol 84.IT'S A FAT WORLD
Vol 85.MAGICAL HAT
Vol 86.WHIRLPOOL
Vol 87.MAGICAL STAIRWAY
Vol 88.BUBBLE BURST
Vol 89.EGG'S TRA LARGE
Vol 90.PYAARE'S SHOP
Vol 91.CROOKED RULER
Vol 92.CRASH
CHHOTA BHEEM AND KRISHNA (SPECIAL EDITION)
PATALI PUTRA (SPECIAL EDITION)
MAYANAGARI (SPECIAL EDITION)
THE RISE OF KIRMADA (SPECIAL EDITION)
DHOLAKPUR TO KATHMANDU (SPECIAL EDITION)
CHHOTA BHEEM AND THE CURSE OF DAMYAAN (MOVIE EDITION)
CHHOTA BHEEM AND THE THRONE OF BALI (MOVIE EDITION)

Special Edition

PATALI PUTRA

Special Edition

MAYANAGARI

Special Edition

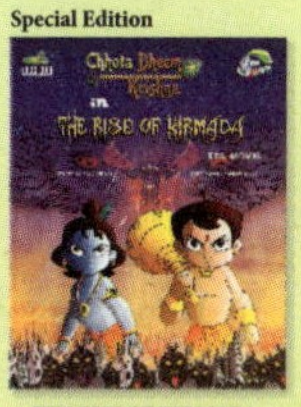

THE RISE OF KIRMADA

Movie Edition

CHHOTA BHEEM AND THE CURSE OF DAMYAAN

Movie Edition

CHHOTA BHEEM AND THE THRONE OF BALI

Movie Edition

MIGHTY RAJU RIO CALLING